Superfoods Recipes: Chicken Soup Recipes For Cold Recovery, Healthy Chicken Noodle Soup Recipes, Holistic Healing Chicken Recipes & Homemade Healing Noodle Soup With Chicken

Juliana Baltimoore

Published by InfinitYou, 2017.

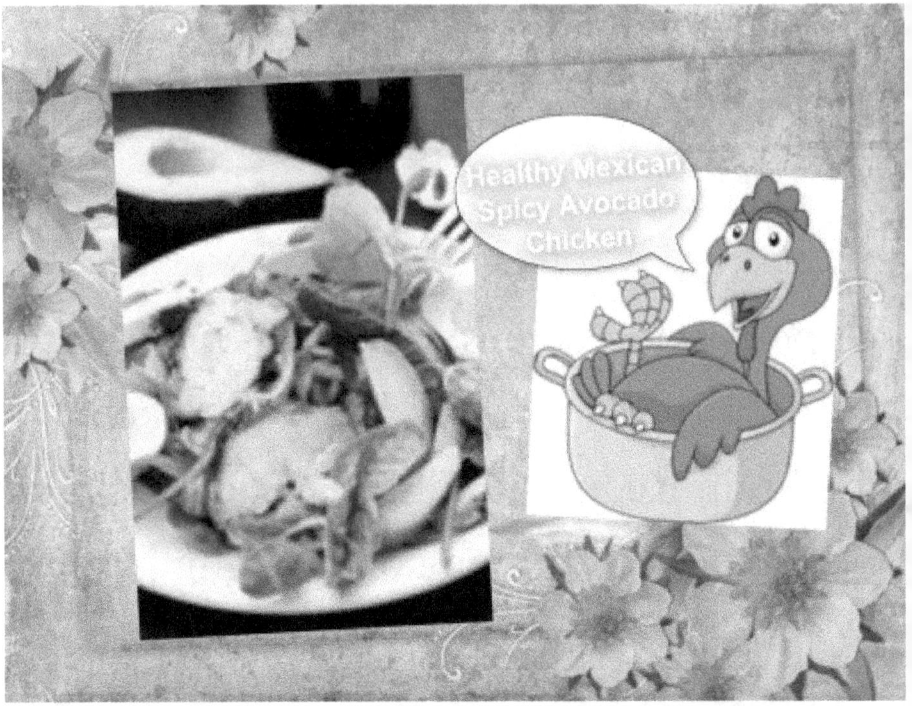
Healthy Mexican Spicy Avocado Chicken

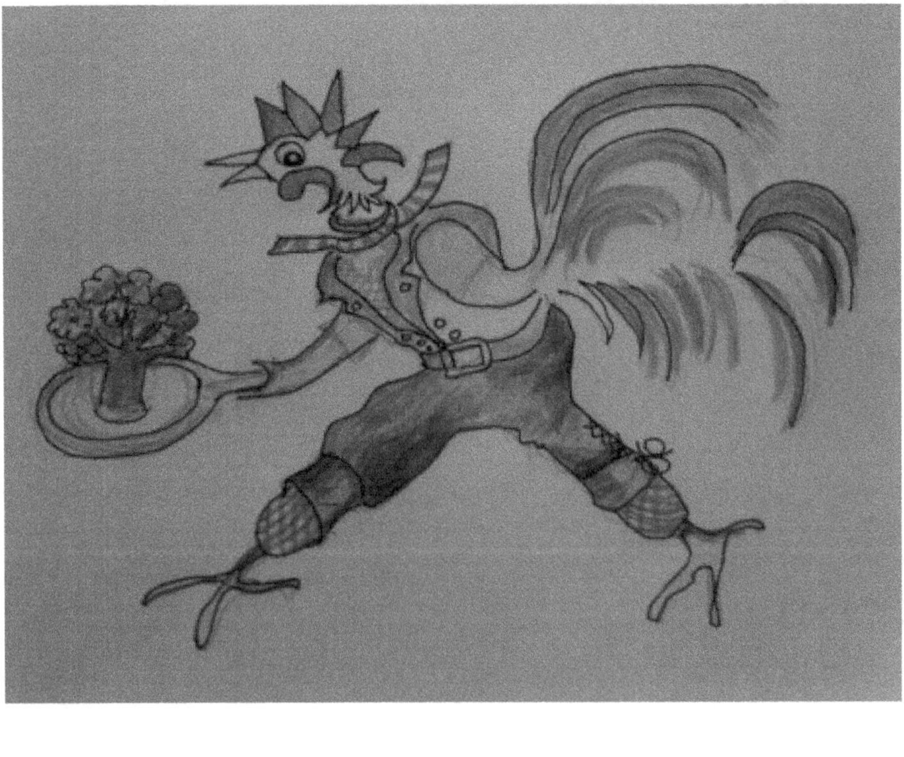

Proven & Tested Cock Soup

Copyright 2017, InfinitYou

ALL RIGHTS RESERVED. One or more global copyright treaties protect the information in this book. This book is not intended to provide exact details or advice. This report is for informational purposes only. Author reserves the right to make any changes necessary to maintain the integrity of the information held within. This book is not presented as legal or accounting advice. All rights reserved, including the right of reproduction in whole or in part in any form. No parts of this book may be reproduced in any form without written permission of the copyright owner.

NOTICE OF LIABILITY

In no event shall the author or the publisher be responsible or liable for any loss of profits or other commercial or personal damages, including but not limited to special incidental, consequential, or any other damages, in connection with or arising out of furnishing, performance or use of this book.

© 2018 InfinitYou

My Favorite Quote About Healthy Eating

Buddha (c. 563 BC to 483 BC) – a spiritual teacher from ancient India and founder of Buddhism

"To keep the body in good health is a duty, otherwise we shall not be able to keep our mind strong and clear"

Introduction

Are you ready to discover these amazing & healthy rare delicacies of cock and hens and learn in a fun and delicious way to eating healthy chicken and cock meat that will boost your vitality and health?

These healthy and tasty recipes are accompanying you through this "Nourishing Journey".

The recipes are all newbie friendly and uncomplicated so that even a new cook can get the health benefits out of these cock and chicken recipes.

These are the type of recipes that you want to have in store for yourself and your family because all these recipes deliver how to prepare cock and chicken the right way!

I am even using these cock and chicken recipes to overcome a wide variety of health conditions including candida albicans, multiple food allergies, acne, morning sickness, male infertility and impotence, low immunity, lack of appetite in elderly and convalescents, overweight and obesity and more.

Each healthy chicken and cock recipe includes a list of ingredients and gives you the instructions to follow. The recipes are easy to follow and do not take longer than a quick preparation time. The cooking time is no longer than 1 hour so that you can still use the cooking time and do some productive things in the meantime.

I am sharing these amazingly tasty and healthy chicken and cock recipes for the very first time so you can take advantage and be able to get started with nourishing your body and brain the right way.

Ultimately, I have written this book to make you aware of the many advantage that come with these healthy chicken and cock recipes.

Tap into some of these powerful health benefits of chicken and cock meat because cocks have been used to heal many sicknesses over the centuries.

These recipes should give you enough ideas to get you started with eating more of these delicious and healthy chicken and cock meals.

If you are looking to become healthier, make sure to integrate more and more of these healthy recipes or similar ingredients to these recipes into your weekly meal plan.

Everybody has a different goal and you can consume more or less of these healthy dishes depending on your personal situation, your goal and your lifestyle.

One thing is for sure, if you get yourself into the habit of consuming more of these healthy ingredients, you will empower and transform your body and mind with the result of a healthier, cleaner, fitter and leaner you.

I hope you like the paintings and the art that is included with each individual recipe. My husband who I call loving words like "Nutty" (because he just loves to say out loud the expression "From Soup To Nuts" and he kind of makes me go nuts with this habit) is an artist and a chef and he hand painted each illustration to show his own love for cocks and hens the "Nutty" way. I hope that you love the heart-warming art that comes with each recipe so that you get some food for the soul at the same time as you prepare these lovely dishes.

Anyways, we decided to include these funny heart-warming illustrations of my husband because we feel that art and food connects well and fun always helps boost the immune system.

I hope you enjoy the book and I hope that you will get lots of inspirational moments out of it.

Let's start the fun journey of hens, roosters and immune boosters!

Welcome to a new and healthy lifestyle with cock and chicken recipes!

Amazing Healthy Recipe 1: Beer Can Chicken Grill Recipe

Did you know that beer and hops contain many health benefits?

Hops have been traditionally used for a huge variety of all these health benefits. Research has confirmed these findings on a scientific level, too.

Among the health benefits from hops researchers found out that hops help relaxation and can work as a sleep inducer. Hops have an estrogenic, anti inflammatory, anti antioxidant activity. Hop is also good for the anti tumor properties.

This is why my first recipe includes the ingredient of beer.

I call it the "Beer Can Chicken". It is so simple, delicious and healthy on top of it because all the ingredients like beer, garlic and olive oil that are included are known for their health benefits.

Health Benefits of Beer and Hops:
Sleep & Relaxation Inducing Health Benefits
Anti inflammatory Health Benefit
Health Benefits for Menopause Symptoms
Anti cancer Benefits
Anti HIV-1 Viral Activity
Anti Acne Benefits
Weight Loss Benefits
Health Benefits for Chronic Liver Diseases

If you are in the mood for a tasty barbeque, all you really need is a four pound chicken, a beer and some of your favorite spices. Set your fire and in an hour or so you will have this delicious grilled beer can chicken that is falling off the bone because it is so juicy and tender.

Some people call this beer in the rear chicken but no matter what name you are going to call it this is the most tasty barbecued (BBQ) chicken around. Just a few minutes of preparation and then you can take the following hour off while it cooks!

Ingredients

1 whole chicken from the farmer's market and biological if possible and around four pounds in weight

The chicken has to be washed and dried and all the giblets removed from the inside

1 of your favorite brands of beers (I love to use Heineken). You need to use one can of beer

2 fresh cloves of garlic

2 teaspoons of original Italian olive oil

2-3 tablespoons of seasoned salt or you can also use dry rub of your choice

2 fresh oranges. The oranges need to be sliced in halfes and slice one half into quarters

Preparation

Heat your griddle to middle heat.

Rub the chicken entirely with olive oil. Then dust the rub or seasoned salt all over the bird, including the hole.

Open the can of your favorite beer and drop half of it. Place the garlic cloves inside the can. Place the chicken on top of the beer can by holding the chicken up and press the can into the hole. Stick one quarter of the orange in top of the chicken.

Balance the chicken on the can of beer and place on the griddle over indirect middle heat. Cover and cook for roughly one and a half hours till thermometer reads 165F and the juice of the chicken runs clear when it is poked with a fork.

Place the orange slices next to the chicken and without further delay. Cover them and grill them for roughly 3-5minutes.

Remove the chicken from griddle and let the chicken rest on the lager can for roughly 10-15 minutes before trying to take away the can and slice the bird.

Before serving, squeeze 2 of the orange halves on top of the chicken and serve the others on the side.

Ensure the bird isn't placed over direct heat on the griddle.

Turn on one side of the griddle and place the bird on the other side.

Tips:

If employing a charcoal griddle push the coals to the side and cook the bird on the other, or push the coals to both sides and cook the bird in the middle. Be certain to let the chicken cool for no less than 10-15 minutes before making an attempt to take away the beer can.

BBQ tongs will make this job less complicated and you feel like you are on a mini vacation!

Enjoy your tender and delicious beer chicken!

Amazing Healthy Recipe 2: Warm Italian White Bean Salad Pleasure With Cock Junks

The warm Italian white bean salad with cock meat is a pleasure of degustation. I have discovered this cock delicacy the first time in Italy. The Italians love their "Antipasti" (starters) and beans are used in a variety of Italian starter dishes.

Just remember, it is important to recall whenever you are making beans that the initial soaking water must be drained but also rinsed before the actual cooking process begins.

This process helps remove the gassiness from the white beans. You will see that eating beans becomes a real pleasure like this. Who needs a gassy and embarrassing experience anyway?

Ingredients:

1/2 lb white beans (use organic cannellini beans or navy, whatever you prefer is fine). The beans must be soaked in fresh source water or filtered water

2 cups of cock meat left over from making stock. The cock must be chopped

1 thinly sliced shallot

1/2 cup of organic celery

1/4 cup of Italian red wine or you can use some sherry vinegar

1/4 cup or more of Italian extra virgin olive oil

1 small bunch of parsley. Chop it

Sea salt and organic white pepper

Preparation:

After draining and rinsing the white beans, place the beans in a pot and cover them with at least 2 inches of filtered water or fresh spring water. Bring it to a boil and cook it for about an hour. Cook it until the beans are soft and make sure they do not become mushy.

Drain the beans and place them in a bowl. While the beans are still warm, add organic shallot, organic celery, red wine vinegar, and the Italian olive oil, salt and pepper.

Toss everything.

Add the chopped parsley and the cold cock meat.

Toss it again.

If the mixture seems dry make sure to add some more olive oil to your liking.

Serve this white bean cock salad slightly warm with a crusty all organic whole grain bread or serve it on some lettuce leaves or Italian arugula salad leaves.

Some Tips for the soaking process:

A quicker process to soak your white beans is to place them in a pot covered with filtered or source water.

Next, bring the water to a boil for around 5 minutes.

Turn off the heat and next add a pinch of baking soda to it.

Allow the soaked beans to sit there for an hour.

The last step is to drain.

Proceed with the recipe as instructed.

Amazing Healthy Recipe 3: Home Remedy Cock Broth

Today experts know that cock has some powerful and healing medicinal and digestive effects. This is why I want to share my next recipe with you. This cock recipe is very medicinal in effect and it helps the digestive system while boosting up the immune system.

This is a dish that Mediterranean inhabitants enjoy for a lunch starter.

It is also perfect for illnesses that relate to appetite loss and weight loss. It stimulates the stomach to want more food. It energizes and vitalizes the whole body and makes the weak stronger. Keep this medicinal cock broth ritual if you are feeling down or sick and within a few days your mobility is going to improve. You will see that your appetite is going to come back, too!

Ingredients: (serves 4)
    6 cups of cock stock, strained
    1/4 cup of broken vermicellis (Italian Noodles)
    2 tablespoons of freshly chopped parsley, chop it very fine
    Sea salt

Preparation:

Heat up your cock stock in a medium sized pot. Next add the vermicelli and cook your broth according to the directions.

    Usually the cooking time does not take more than three to four minutes.

    The last step is to add the fresh parsley and some sea salt to our liking.

    Serve this healthy cock delicacy steamy hot and enjoy!

Amazing Healthy Recipe 4: Proven & Tested Cock Soup

Did you know that cock has become very popular over the past few years for its healthy benefits?

This cock soup is so simple, delicious and healthy on top of it.

Health Benefits Of Cock:
Heals candida albicans
Good for multiple food allergies
Heals bleeding eczemas
Heals acne problems
Good for morning sickness
Helps male infertility and impotence
Helps boost low immunity
Helps lack of appetite in elderly and convalescents
Helps overweight and obesity with weight loss

SUPERFOODS RECIPES: CHICKEN SOUP RECIPES FOR COLD RECOVERY, HEALTHY CHICKEN NOODLE SOUP RECIPES, HOLISTIC HEALING CHICKEN RECIPES & HOMEMADE HEALING NOODLE SOUP WITH CHICKEN

Helps pregnant women benefit and ensures the health of unborn newborns

If you are in the mood for this healthy cock soup or if you are feeling sick and down this soup is all you need. It is going to boost your immune system. In this case I recommend eating it at night and having a full night of sleep. The next morning you feel energized and full of vitality.

Make this dish whenever you feel that you are coming down with the flu. This is a preventive home remedy that will keep you fit around the year. Make sure to include it in your weekly meal plan and you do not have to see the doctor for a long time!

It is the most healthy and easy to make home remedy that you can treat yourselves with whenever you feel you need a little energy and if you need an immunity booster.

All you really need is a whole cock and some veggies. Make sure you get everything the organic fashion.

In around an hour you will have the most delicious and tasty cock soup in front of you and this is going to be a delicious feast.

Just a few minutes of preparation time and then you can take the following hour off while it cooks for you!

Ingredients: (makes 4 quarts)

1 whole cock, preferably with head and feet on

2 organic carrots that are peeled and sliced

1 large organic onion, in very thin slices

3 cups of organic and assorted diced vegetables. You can use veggies like organic string beans, organic potatoes, organic leafy cooking greens, organic turnips, just get creative here!)

2 organic ribs of celery and chopped in thin pieces

4 quarts of source water or filtered water

1 tablespoon of raw cider vinegar

some sea salt

Preparation:

Place your organic whole cock the cider vinegar and the water into a big stockpot.

Simmer the whole pot for one hour over low heat.

Remove any scum and unappetizing materials that are flowing on the top of the soup and discard it.

Add all veggies to the hot broth and continue to cook it for another hour.

Lastly, lift out the cock and remove the meat from the bones.

Return the cock meat to the pot.

Add sea some sea salt and stir to dissolve it.

Serve this healing broth hot and enjoy!

Amazing Healthy Recipe 5: Cock Lemon Basil Sauce With Tagliatelle

Did you know that most packages of pasta do suggest to serve a quarter pound of pasta per person. No wonder why people are having health and weight problems!

This suggestion is way too much and totally ridiculous.

Someone who knows a little bit about Italian cooking knows that a typical Italian rarely eats large portions of pasta because the Past is served after the Anitpasti and before the main dish.

My suggestion is to follow this delicious dish with a refreshing composed garden salad or arugula salad with balsamico dressing and a nice glass of red or white wine.

SUPERFOODS RECIPES: CHICKEN SOUP RECIPES FOR COLD RECOVERY, HEALTHY CHICKEN NOODLE SOUP RECIPES, HOLISTIC HEALING CHICKEN RECIPES & HOMEMADE HEALING NOODLE SOUP WITH CHICKEN

Ingredients: (Serves 8 persons)

1 pound of dried tagliatelle. Make sure to cook the tagliatelle accordingly. It is written on the package so just follow the manufacturer's directions.

2 tablespoons of organic butter

3 organic shallots that are finely chopped

2 cups of heavy cream (not ultra pasteurized and organic if you can)

1 pound of cock meat that you reserved from making stock, the cock needs to be chopped

The juice of an organic lemon

Sea salt and ground white pepper to your liking

Preparation:

In a large sauté pan, go ahead and melt the organic butter over medium heat. Add the organic chopped shallots and cook them in the pan until they have a translucent color.

Next add your heavy cream. Bring the mixture to a boiling point.
Allow your lemon sauce to thicken slightly.
Next, add the cock meat and the fresh lemon juice to the mix.
Thicken the lemon sauce a bit more if you like.
Lastly, add the freshly drained and not rinsed linguine to the lemon sauce.
Stir to blend everything.

If the sauce is still to thick, use a little bit of your linguine's cooking water to make the sauce a little thinner. Just a touch because the sauce does not need to be too liquid!

Serve the Tagliatelle with Lemon Basil Cock sauce steamy hot and serve with a glass of red or white Italian wine!

Amazing Healthy Recipe 6: Brazilian Chicken With Black Beans Vodoo

I love the Brazilian cooking, but I also know that Brazilian food is very heavy and contains lots of calories. Not only do I want to look good in my bikini this summer, but I want to share another great tasting chicken recipe with you that passes the food lover approval because the deliciousness is key to my recipes.

I have turned my favorite Brazilian chicken recipe from a heavy and fat pork recipe into a healthy, lean and tasty poultry delicacy. My recipe is a lighter versions of this popular Brazilian dish while still giving it the alluring flavor.

Brazilian cooking remains one of the least known, and most interesting, cuisines thanks to its combination of Portuguese, African and native Indian influences. Its unfamiliarity comes from the lack of a significant Brazilian population in the United States. This also explains why unique ingredients that some dishes require are almost unavailable.

You can still get the ingredients online or at some speciality food markets.

Anyways, I fixed the heaviness of the ingredients and only use simple-to-find ingredients so that you do not have to go through this painful process.

I call the dish "Brazilian Cock With Black Beans Vodoo" which is a stew called feijoada (fey-zhoo-ah-dah) in Brazilian language. It is one of Brazil's elemental dishes.

Instead of the fatty pork Brazilians normally use, I am using lean chicken. Skinless thighs are ideal, but I find that bone in breast works well, too.

I also streamlined the cooking time because who has hours to pass in the kitchen?

This is why I am using canned (but still organic) beans rather than dried beans for this dish.

The bay leaf, allspice and fresh oranges served with the dish, makes this the perfect healthy Brazilian flavor feijoada!

Ingredients: (Serves 6 persons)

2 tablespoons of canola oil

2 pounds of skinless chicken thighs with the bone or skinless chicken breast with ribs or a combination

1/2 cup of fat free and reduced sodium chicken broth

1¼ cups of chopped organic onion

3/4 cup of chopped organic celery

3/4 cup of chopped organic green bell peppers

3/4 cup of chopped organic scallions, the green and the white parts

3 organic garlic cloves, chopped

2 bay leaves (organic if possible)

1/4 teaspoon of freshly ground nutmeg (organic if possible)

2 (15 oz. cans) of black organic beans, already rinsed and drained

Sea Salt

Freshly ground black pepper (organic if possible)

1/8 tsp. of cayenne pepper (organic if possible)
2 tablespoons of chopped organic flat leaf parsley
1 large organic navel orange, cut the orange in 6 wedges

Preparation:

In a large Dutch oven, go ahead and heat one tablespoon of the oil over a medium high heat.

Next, add the chicken and cook it until it is golden brown and for four minutes on each side.

Transfer the chicken to a large bowl.

Cover the bowl with foil.

Add some broth and scrap the bottom of the pot while it boils and gather up all browned particles and pieces.

Next, add broth to the chicken.

Seal the foil tightly over the bowl and set the chicken aside.

Using paper towel, wipe out the pot

Return the pot to a medium high heat and add the remaining oil.

Add the organic onion, the organic celery, the organic green pepper and the organic scallions to the pot and cook.

Stir occasionally, until you get a soft texture (around 5 minutes).

Add some organic garlic and cook.

Stir for 1 minute.

Add the bay leaves and sprinkle some nutmeg over the veggies.

Arrange the chicken pieces over the vegetables, reserving liquid in the bowl.

Spread the beans over the chicken.

Pour the liquid from the bowl over the beans.

Cover and simmer until the chicken thighs are soft and tender and are falling apart (around 30-35 minutes).

If using chicken breast, cook it until it is white in the center and at the thickest part (around 20-25 minutes).

To serve the dish, divide the chicken among six plates.

Remove the bay leaf.

Mix to combine beans and vegetables. Season to your own taste with salt, pepper and cayenne.

Next, spoon two thirds cups of beans and veggies alongside the chicken and the liquid from the pot over the chicken.

Garnish with fresh organic parsley and some decorative orange wedges.

Serve this Brazilian chicken dish hot and enjoy this delicacy!

Tips:

Most of the time when I am making this dish, I have leftovers. I am keeping the leftovers tightly covered in the fridge. I do not keep it for more than 2 days.

This is a perfect dish for a convivial summer supper with your family and friends!

Amazing Healthy Recipe 7: Healthy Mexican Spicy Avocado Chicken

Here is one last thought for you when it comes to the health benefits of chicken.

The skinless chicken breast (the white meat only) is one of the most protein packed and leanest health foods you can eat to keep your body fit and full of energy.

Some people think it is boring or tasteless to eat the white chicken meat, but nothing can be farer from the truth.

Here's how to keep white chicken meat one of the most delicious and healthy dishes that you can get your hands on.

This spicy Mexican avocado chicken dish is a good source of potassium, folate and monounsaturated fatty acids.

Some more Health Benefits of Chicken:

Eating lean chicken meat helps to lose weight and helps with weight control

Niacin protects the body from cancer

Selenium, which is an element that helps promote thyroid hormone metabolism and ultimately helps control the metabolic pathways

Anti oxidant helps to defend the immunity and immune system of the body

Eating lean chicken helps activate cells and molecules from the Vitamin B6 components of the chicken meat this in turn forms the cellular aspect of the body which repairs the blood vessels

Phosphorus, a unique component helps the body to have strong muscles and bones that may eventually ensure the better function of our inner organs, too

The lean chicken meat also stimulates the growth and development of the body and helps with the most important body parts, for example, unleashing energy functions

SUPERFOODS RECIPES: CHICKEN SOUP RECIPES FOR COLD RECOVERY, HEALTHY CHICKEN NOODLE SOUP RECIPES, HOLISTIC HEALING CHICKEN RECIPES & HOMEMADE HEALING NOODLE SOUP WITH CHICKEN

Ingredients:

4 small organic chicken breast fillets
1 tablespoon of sweet paprika
Pinch of organic cayenne pepper
1 organic avocado. Cube the flesh
2 tablespoons of organic lime juice
1 organic green chili. Make sure to remove the seeds and slice it lengthways. Slice it very thin
2 tablespoons of fresh and organic chives
Traditional organic olive oil - or organic olive oil spray
0.5 pounds steamed organic green beans

Preparation:

First, cut each chicken breast into 3 thin escalopes.
Toss them in the combined paprika and cayenne to lightly coat the escalopes. Set them aside.
Place the organic avocado, the fresh lime, the chili and the chives in a bowl.
Season and stir gently to combine everything.
Set it aside.
Heat a large pan over high heat and spray the pan with the Olive oil. Cook your organic chicken escalopes in 2 batches and for 2 minutes on each side until they are cooked.
Next, halve each piece on an angle.
Serve the chicken on the salsa and drizzle the dish with any resting juices.
You can serve the dish with a light composed salad of greens or a bowl of legumes.

Conclusion

I have a lot of fun experimenting with these healthy and delicious cock and chicken recipes, and I hope that these recipes are getting you started with your own goals and of how you want to use these recipes, too.

There's a lot of satisfaction when you stumble on a healthy chicken recipe that tastes fantastic at the same time. It's more gratifying if the recipe is quick to make, easy to make, tasty and healthy at the same time.

Use these recipes as a starting point and make your own experiments and experiences with them and make sure to jot down notes when you make changes to the recipes!

There is little worse than playing around and making a great and healthy chicken and cock recipe only to realize you can't remember precisely what you probably did. By making recipes that you adore, you'll find yourself anticipating your meal plans in a more effective and productive fashion.

Since they're so high in nourishment, you will begin to feel more fit.

If you're like me, you may also find that the more that you replace unhealthy food options with these amazing tasting healthy recipes, the more that you will begin to enjoy healthier food options like salads and fresh items. Convenience foods like potato chips will begin to taste tasteless.

The additional energy you get from the vegetable, legumes and plant based side dishes will also assist you in working out more.

All this mixed will assist in making your efforts a big success!

I attempted to make this cock and chicken recipe book as fascinating, inspiring, interesting and encouraging for you so that you really take action and tap into the health benefits.

Just keep the book in your kitchen right next to your working table and go through one recipe at a time and as you progress with it.

The book is intended to be used in an interactive and stimulating fashion and to empower you to take action at the same time.

Ultimately, the goal of this book is to lead you to a healthy lifestyle that in this case includes healthy chicken and cock food choices.

Once you have shed the pounds or are satisfied with the healthy benefits that you were looking to tap into it is important to keep making and consuming these healthy dishes.

SUPERFOODS RECIPES: CHICKEN SOUP RECIPES FOR COLD RECOVERY, HEALTHY CHICKEN NOODLE SOUP RECIPES, HOLISTIC HEALING CHICKEN RECIPES & HOMEMADE HEALING NOODLE SOUP WITH CHICKEN

Including these healthy chicken and cock dishes into your meal plans and including these healthy recipes into your lifestyle is what you should be aiming for as your ultimate goal, too.

Once you are at the level of including these healthy recipes into your daily lifestyle and once you are successful with keeping and maintaining your weight and your vitality by choosing these healthy food choices, you have achieved your ultimate goal which is making healthy eating a natural habit.

The plan of the Smoothie diet, however, is very kind and intelligent because it follows the rules of the body. It nourishes and energizes the body throughout the day with all the beneficial ingredients and nutrients that are beneficial for the body and mind and it keeps your body and mind productive all the time.

I hope you will use and consume the content whenever you need some inspiration and motivation for making some healthy chicken and cock recipes that are either helping you with your weight loss goal, or healing process or that you just like to include into your daily meal plan because you are already in the habit of living the healthy and fit lifestyle.

Remember, all you have to do is open the book and start with the first recipe preparation. Go through all of them and apply them on a daily basis as you see fit and depending on the health, healing or weight loss goals that you are looking to achieve.

You will soon see for yourself that making these chicken and cock recipes is a lot of fun plus a lifestyle with healthy food is going to make you very happy, lean and clean.

To your success with Chicken, Roosters and Immunity Boosters!

About the Publisher

InfinitYou is a hybrid general interest trade publisher. One of the first of its kind InfinitYou publishes physical books, electronic books, and audiobooks in various genres. Our publications are meant to educate, edify and entertain readers of all walks of life from babies to the elderly.

Home to more than twenty imprints such as Infinit Baby, Infinit Kids, Infinit Girl, Infinit Boy, Infinit Coloring, Infinit Swear Words, Infinit Activities, Infinit Productivity, Infinit Cat, Infinit Dog, Infinit Love, Infinit Family, Infinit Survival, Infinit Health, Infinit Beauty, Infinit Spirituality, Infinit Lifestyle, Infinit Wealth, Infinit Romance, and lots more.

www.ingramcontent.com/pod-product-compliance
Lightning Source LLC
LaVergne TN
LVHW012131070526
838202LV00056B/5947